Amy Carmichael

I Come Quietly to Meet You

Amy Carmichael

I Come Quietly to Meet You

AN INTIMATE JOURNEY IN GOD'S PRESENCE

BETHANYHOUSE

Minneapolis, Minnesota

I Come Quietly to Meet You
Copyright © 1991, 2005
David Hazard

Cover design by Eric Walljasper

Previously published title: *You Are My Hiding Place*

Unless otherwise identified, Scripture quotations are from the HOLY BIBLE, NEW INTERNATIONAL VERSION.® Copyright © 1973, 1978, 1984 by International Bible Society. Used by permission of Zondervan Publishing House. All rights reserved.

The selections of Amy Carmichael's writings used in this volume are from the following titles: *Thou Givest, They Gather; His Thoughts Said. . .; Rose from Brier; Figures of the True; If; God's Missionary; Gold by Moonlight; Candles in the Dark; Edges of His Ways.*

All portions are used by permission of Christian Literature Crusade (CLC), Fort Washington, Pa. No selection may be reproduced without written permission from CLC. Excerpts taken from *Edges of His Ways* and *Candles in the Dark* are reprinted by special permission of the Society for Promoting Christian Knowledge. Further reprint permission must be obtained from S.P.C.K.: Holy Trinity Church, Marylebone Road, London, NW1 4DU.

Prayers following the devotional selections are by David Hazard.

Published by Bethany House Publishers
11400 Hampshire Avenue South
Bloomington, Minnesota 55438

Bethany House Publishers is a division of
Baker Publishing Group, Grand Rapids, Michigan.

Printed in the United States of America

ISBN   978-0-7642-0045-8

In keeping with biblical principles of creation stewardship, Baker Publishing Group advocates the responsible use of our natural resources. As a member of the Green Press Initiative, our company uses recycled paper when possible. The text paper of this book is comprised of 30% post-consumer waste.

green press INITIATIVE

Library of Congress Cataloging-in-Publication Data

Carmichael, Amy, 1867–1951.
   [You are my hiding place]
   I come quietly to meet you : an intimate journey in God's presence : devotional readings / Amy Carmichael ; arranged by David Hazard.
       p.   cm.
   Originally published: You are my hiding place, c1991, in series: Rekindling the inner fire.
       Summary: "These devotional writings by Amy Carmichael offer readers uplifting times with God, showing them how to find safety in Him, live honestly before Him, and receive peace as they live in His presence"—Provided by publisher.
   ISBN 0-7642-0045-3 (pbk.)
   1. Spiritual life—Christianity. I. Hazard, David. II. Title.
   BV4501.3.C375   2005
   242—dc22   2005020513

To Jim and Millie Hertzler

Thank you
for helping me to find
"the hiding place."

CONTENTS

AMY CARMICHAEL

*You are my hiding place; you will protect me from
trouble and surround me with songs of deliverance.*

PSALM 32:7

"Amy Carmichael was born in Northern Ireland, and after a brief period in Japan, arrived in India on 9 November 1895 as a [Keswick Convention] missionary. She never left India until her death on 18 January 1951. . . ."

So begins one collection of Amy Carmichael's writings, *Candles in the Dark*: But what a clear-shining expanse of life lies hidden between those two sentences!

Early on, Amy Carmichael seems to have learned a spiritual secret that caused her spirit, if anything, to blaze even brighter in spite of the many difficult circumstances—friends would misunderstand and fail to support her work, physical danger threatened, and injury and pain would pin her to a bed for the last years of her life.

Through it all, she seems to have dug to find deeper and deeper spiritual gold in these words:

Set your minds on things above, not on earthly things. For you died, and your life is now hidden with Christ in God. (Colossians 3:3)

Amy never understood this promise to mean a Christian is like a jewel in a velvet case, coddled and protected from every scratch. To her, the Christian life was more like being made a warrior and learning to suit herself in spiritual armor, ready to do battle.

And for Amy, "hidden with Christ in God," the battles would be great and hostile.

Arriving in India in her late-twenties, she set out on her mission, travelling throughout the state of Tamil Nadu. For six years, moving among the small rural villages, she evangelized in the company of Indian Christian women. Great numbers were drawn to the light of Christ, not just by the teaching, but also by the love and simple goodness in these women. The bitter anger of Hindu priests was only held back—and barely—by the ruling British administration.

Then in 1901, a terrified little girl was brought to Amy at her mission compound in Dohnavur. Only seven years old, this child was one of thousands and thousands dedicated as infants to service in the temples of Hindu gods. Among other horrors, she was to be made a temple prostitute. The child could not be sent back—despite the tremendous danger of keeping her.

Some Christians disagreed with Amy's decision to provide this child—and others who escaped into her safe-keeping—with a home and love and a Christian upbringing. "Shouldn't missionaries just evangelize, and leave the rest alone? Why fight a centuries-old custom when you're sure to make enemies, and most likely fail?" Despite death threats against Amy and the mission, the British administration remained silent on the issue.

As danger mounted, Amy had to "tuck herself into God," as she put it. Fortunately, others heard of the child-rescue work and came to reinforce her.

And so the mission at Dohnavur grew. Eventually, hundreds of girls—and boys too—would join the large "family" that became known as Dohnavur Fellowship—men, women, and children learning together how to come daily under the protection of God, with need and fear surrounding on all sides.

Then came personal tragedy.

In 1932, Amy experienced a crippling fall. Internal damages were severe and left her in terrible pain. She expected to recover in weeks, perhaps months—unaware at first that she would virtually never leave her bed again. Even as the crushing truth of it dawned, her eyes were already fixed on a different light: the light of God's presence and His goodness.

Even through constant pain—her "fetters of iron"—Amy continued to pour forth devotional writings, brilliant in spiritual passion and plain wisdom.

Effortlessly, she cites from numerous Bible versions and commentaries, some no longer in use. She also quotes at will from a procession of leading Christian voices, some of her spiritual "mentors," that come to us down through the ages: from Julian of Norwich, to Alfred the Great, to George Herbert.

To read Amy Carmichael is to find your own spirit rekindled by the intensity of her "vision" of God. At the bedrock of her faith lie these immovable principles:

- God is, first and always, a loving Father.
- Everything that comes to us is for our *good*, because it comes from a good Father, in whom there is no darkness.
- When we come to know our "Father of Lights"— when we "tuck" ourselves into God by trusting Him as little children—He will carry us through.

May you find, in the company of Amy Carmichael, the burst of joy that comes when we can say to God from the depths of our being, "I come quietly to meet you."

David Hazard

1

LEARNING TO LIVE
"AT HOME"

You are my hiding place;
you will protect me from trouble
and surround me with songs of deliverance.

PSALM 32:7

I think distractions in prayer are often because we have let ourselves wander too far from the things that matter most. And so we slip into an easily interrupted, easily distracted frame of mind.

We need to live more at home.

"In him we live and move and have our being" (Acts 17:28). This means, simply, *God is our home.*

Home of my heart, lest I forget
    My redemption's cost to Thee,
Let my earliest thought be set
    Upon Thy Calvary.

Do you see what I mean? These words, which center

my attention on what matters most, speak of something that I cannot drop out of my day without great loss to me.

I know without question that an earnest "look" at Calvary does more to help our life of prayer than we imagine:

> *So shall the sayings of my mouth, and the meditation of my heart, be pleasing continually before Thee, O Lord my helper and my Redeemer.* (Psalm 19:14 SEPTUAGINT)

EDGES OF HIS WAYS: P. 160

MY FATHER, SOMETHING inward tells me I have been living scattered. Sometimes anxious. Restless. Distracted. Wandering inside.

I fix my eyes upon the cross now—upon the post and crossbeam which became my one bridge back to your side.

And I lift my eyes beyond the cross, to the One who sits beside you—to Jesus, the Risen One! My Lord, my brother, with arms outstretched in welcome. Calling to me:

"Come home."

I come, Father, to hide myself in you.

2

LEANING

The Lord spoke to me, like a firm grasp of the hand.
ISAIAH 8:11, ROTHERHAM

Blessed be the Lord our God, who does—if we speak the honest truth—cause His word to come to us in just this way: like a strong hand reaching out for us to take hold of firmly, and to take hold of us.

Sometimes this firm grasp comes as He opens our understanding to a *single word*. His hand has grasped me, in recent days, as my understanding opens up to the word *trust*.

Trust, I have learned, means: *to lean on, to place the weight of my confidence upon* (Young's Analytical Concordance). . . . And after this discovery, I've found many verses in the Psalms that provide great comfort when translated in this way. For instance, "I have trusted in [leaned on, placed confidence in] your lovingkindness" (Psalm 13:5).

So I may say: That lovingkindness which has loved

me with an everlasting love, which forgives and cleanses and will never tire of me—*that* lovingkindness, Lord, I lean on.

We know that this is not objectionable to the Lord, that He in fact welcomes it. As David sang: "The Lord's unfailing love surrounds the man who [leans on] him" (Psalm 32:10).

Doesn't this tell us something about the love of God—and isn't it just like Him to let us know that He *wants* us to lean on, not only His lovingkindness, but on His very *self*? Consider these words, which will further open your understanding:

Now there was leaning on Jesus' bosom one of his disciples whom Jesus loved. (John 13:23, KJV)

Whoso leaneth on the Lord, happy is he. (Proverbs 16:20, KJV)

He is indeed happy with us!
Now see what happens when we lean on Him:

Cause me to hear . . . for on thee do I lean. (Psalm 143:8, KJV)

It was when John was leaning that he heard the Lord's answer to the question that troubled others.
And this wonderful promise, so often repeated:

What time I am afraid, I will lean on thee. (Psalm 56:3, KJV)

I will lean, and not be afraid. (Isaiah 12:2)

Thou wilt keep him in perfect peace . . . because he leans on thee. . . . Lean on the Lord forever: for the Lord Jehovah is everlasting strength. (Isaiah 26:3, 4, KJV)

It is marvelous to me that God's Spirit led the writers of these words to the same special verb, *to lean*. By one simple word, He means to show us so clearly that it is never anything *in* us that accounts for the Lord's goodness *to* us. Everything we are given is all from Him.

The Lord is my strength and my shield; my heart leans on him and I am helped. Therefore my heart greatly rejoices, and with my song will I praise him! (Psalm 28:7)

May the Lord of love make this word of His to be "like a firm grasp of the hand" to you today.

THOU GIVEST—THEY GATHER: PP. 1–2

MY FATHER, YOU welcome me into your presence—and that's a wonder in itself. More than I can imagine. Then you invite me to lean against you . . . and a bolt of self-reliance in me resists.

But I *want* to trust you. To relax the weight of my fears and anxieties against you. To rest, to know how fully trustworthy you are. Help me, Father.

I reach for your hand, feel your firm grip . . . and I lean my weight against you now.

3

NO INSIGNIFICANT
PEOPLE

My God, with his lovingkindness, will meet me.
PSALM 59:10, REVISED VERSION OF 1901

To some of us, there often comes such a sense of the vastness of things and of our own insignificance that it can be a shaking thing. It can even shake our faith in the truth that our Father regards with compassion even the fall of a single sparrow (Matthew 10:29).

To me, one of the proofs that God's hand is behind and all throughout this marvelous Book we know as the Bible is the way it continually touches upon this very fear in us—the fear that we are so insignificant as to be forgotten. That we are nothing. Unconsciously, His Word meets this fear and answers it—not always by a direct statement, but often by giving a simple, loving little story.

Daniel, for instance, was so overwhelmed by his supernatural vision of the vast majestic march of history and the glory of the Lord that his physical strength vanished—until "a hand touched me" (Daniel 10:8–10).

John, looking through the thin veil of time into eternity, saw his Lord—the Lord he had seen pierced—now holding in His hand seven stars. John declares: "I fell at His feet as though dead." Immediately—just as though this fallen one mattered more than the seven stars, as though there were no stars—"He placed His right hand upon me" (Revelation 1:16–17).

Isn't it beautiful that there was no rebuke at all for their human weakness? And there never is a rebuke for our weaknesses either. "The soul of the wounded calls for help, and God does not regard it as foolish" (Job 24:12, Rotherham).

He comforts. He lays His right hand on the soul wounded by weariness, or fear, or any kind of weakness at all. And He says, as if that one were the only soul in all the universe:

> *O man, greatly beloved, fear not: peace be unto thee. Be strong—yea, be strong!* (Daniel 10:19 ROTHERHAM)

THOU GIVEST—THEY GATHER: PP. 20–21

MY FATHER, AS IF I am the only one in your universe right now . . . as if you are all that matters in mine. . . . Forgive me the days I thought that meeting with you was "insignificant" compared with all I had to do.

I come quietly to meet you, Father . . . needing to be loved . . . and needing to love you.

4

PAUSE

Selah

PSALM 3:2B

Pause is the word the Greek translation of the Bible uses for *selah*. I like to meditate upon the way it occurs for the first time in the Psalms:

> *Many there be which say of my soul, "There is no help for him in God."*
> Selah.
> *But Thou, O Lord, art my helper, my Glory and the lifter of my head!* (Psalm 3:2 SEPTUAGINT).

We have all been subjected to the wearying voices which flood the very atmosphere around us, complaining, "There is no help...."

These voices murmur and mutter the same words, no matter what the challenge or difficulty may be. "There is no help...."

But because you and I are *in* God, we need not listen:

"There is no help . . . ," they repeat.

Pause.

"But you, O Lord, *are* my helper!"

No matter to us what the voices say. Their words bring only weariness—but with His word comes peace and strength and courage to go on.

This is true, not only with the difficult outward circumstances of our lives, but with inward temptations too. We are tempted. And at once we recall past failures in this same area. This causes us to feel weak and start to fall. The voices within are saying, "There is no help. . . ."

Even these inner struggles may be turned to peace. How? Instead of trying to answer the many voices of the enemy, or arguing with them (we can never win this type of argument), we must do something else.

We *pause.*

We look away from self, away from the enemy. We look *up!*

"There is no help. . . ."

"But *you,* O Lord. . . !"

Some believe that *selah* also signifies a sudden pealing-forth of musical instruments. The pause, then, was for *praise.*

Then let us fill all of our *pauses* with praise! Let us give all that lies within us not to the voices of the enemy, but to pure praise, to pure loving adoration, and to worship from a grateful heart—a heart that is trained to look *up*.

THOU GIVEST—THEY GATHER: P. 18

MY FATHER, TRAIN my soul, today, to *pause*. When the enemy attacks, hurling words that cause me to take my eyes off of you.... When I feel weak, and helpless to do anything but fail again.

I *will* stop.

I *will* look up.

No matter what comes, I will say, "But you, O Lord, are my helper!"

ONE STEP AT A TIME

*Listen to advice and accept instruction, and in the end
you will be wise. Many are the plans in a man's
heart, but it is the Lord's purpose that prevails.*

PROVERBS 19:20–21

I believe that, in guiding us, God deals with us as He dealt with the Israelites as He led them out of Egypt.

The first crossing of the sea was made very easy. The guidance could not have been simpler: The east wind blew and divided the sea before the people had to cross. Not so much as a foot was wet, except perhaps by a wind-driven spray. Moreover, it was impossible, as it were, to disobey, since they were pursued by Pharaoh's chariots and horsemen (Exodus 14).

But how different it was on the second occasion.

The priests had to walk into the strong current of a flooded river and stand still there. What an order to scoff at, and what a sight it would pose to other men! But it was not until they obeyed—without a particle of visible proof that they were doing right—and carried the ark right into the river, that the water rolled back before them (Joshua 3).

So it may be for us as we go on with God.

You and I may be called again and again to walk right into our own "rivers," whatever they may be—to wet our feet in them. We may be called to do what nobody understands except those to whom the word of guidance is given—and with it, His promise too.

But understand this: The word *must* come first, and *also* His promise. You and I must be sure of what we are called to do, with an inward conviction that absolutely nothing can shake. In my own case, again and again, I have had to wet my feet in the water. Only God and those who have to walk in that path know how hard this kind of faith-life can be. But He *does* know. And when the people around us don't hear the words and the voice we have heard, and only say, "It thunders...," then He comes near, and we know Him as we never knew Him before....

If only the next step is clear, then the one thing to do is take it! Don't pledge your Lord or yourself to any steps beyond what you know. You don't see them yet.

Once when I was climbing at night, in a forest before there was a made path, I learned what was meant by the words of Psalm 119:105:

Your word is a lamp to my feet, and a light for my path.

I had only a lantern, and had to hold it very low or I would certainly have slipped on those rough rocks.

We don't walk spiritually by electric light, but by a hand-held lantern. And a lantern shows only the next step—not several steps ahead.

CANDLES IN THE DARK: PP. 41, 43

MY FATHER, THERE are so many paths I could walk—so many ways to choose. And there are certain decisions I must make that lead me around and around, until my heart is in confusion.

Today, I will fix my heart on this truth:

When I feel confused, there will always come a light, held low so that my feet won't stumble—a sure light that will shine on each step of my path.

Thank you, Father, that you will speak the counsels of your word to me.

6

SILENT SONG

Why are you downcast, O my soul?
Why so disturbed within me?
. . . Deep calls to deep . . .
By day the Lord directs his love, at night his song
is with me—a prayer to the God of my life.

PSALM 42:5, 7–8

The son greatly wished to make a "Song of Lovely Things" to sing to his Beloved—but he could not find singing-words.

He heard the voice of his Beloved saying, "You are walking on the road where all who love Me walk. Some of them walked this way singing, and they've left their songs behind them. Find their songs. Sing their words. They will be your song to Me."

But the son became full of grief, because there came a day when he could find no words to sing—neither his own, nor those of others. And yet he wanted with all his heart and soul and mind to ascend to higher places, to stand in the presence of his Beloved. . . .

And He who is love eternal whispered, "Then I, too, will approach you, silent in my love."

And the son entered into this silence, to meet the eternal Beloved there. . . .

After a while there was a sound in the gentle stillness, a voice that whispered, "Even your silence is, to Me, a song of lovely things. . . ."

HIS THOUGHTS SAID . . . HIS FATHER SAID: P. 30

MY FATHER, THERE are reasons why I could feel downcast. When I think about some parts of my life, it's hard to pray—even harder to worship in freedom . . .

. . . relationships that are difficult . . .

. . . dreams and goals that are crumbling . . .

. . . old hurts that wound me over and over. . . .

Some parts of me feel cold and wordless.

Is the problem that I've buried some things deep inside? Are you patiently calling—through days and months—for me to open up to you at some deeper level?

Today, Father, I trust you to go deeper.

7

IF ONLY THERE WERE
MOUNTAINS

*Teach me to number my days aright, that I may gain
a heart of wisdom. . . . Satisfy me in the morning with
your unfailing love, that I may sing for joy
and be glad all my days.*

PSALM 90:12, 14

If you would live in victory over the circumstances, great and small, that come to you each day . . .

. . . and if you want God's life and power to well up from the depths of your being . . .

. . . then you must refuse to be dominated by the *seen* and the *felt*.

You say: "I could climb mountains if God asked me to. That would be a joy!

"But here I stand, on this dreary seashore of my life, looking over this dreary backwash bay and a drearier shoreline—and beyond that, inland, no mountains. Nothing invigorating, or inspiring. Nothing hard enough to inspire *anyone*. . . .

"The whole of my life is like that these days—not hard, just dull. I would have chosen challenging over dull. A challenge that would make me want to achieve at any cost. It's this *useless* feeling that's so devastating."

God says: *"Have you looked up?"*

"Up? I see nothing but a mass of clouds overhead. That's all."

"And nothing beyond those clouds? Look again. Don't you see the hint of light beyond them? Aren't the clouds themselves a marvel of controlled power—reminders of the pillars of cloud and of fire?"

"I must confess, my spiritual vision has failed, what with waiting so long upon my God."

" 'So long. . . ?' You need to grow in patience. For after you have done the will of God, you must learn to wait to receive the full extent of His promise.

"It is written: 'As for me, when I am poor and feeling heavy, your help, O God, will lift me up. I wait patiently, trusting that you will lift me up.'

"And it is also written: 'I will abide in patience, and will praise you more and more.'

"So I ask: Have you tried to face your life—those dull, dreary days—with the lifting power of praise?

"You must look steadfastly through the visible, until the invisible opens up to you."

Figures of the True: p. 5

MY FATHER, SO OFTEN I get weighed down under the demands of my own life. Sometimes I see little purpose in the endless repetition of little duties. Jobs done today, that need doing again tomorrow. . . .

What is it, in the daily work you have given me to do, that is of eternal value to you?

Lift my sights, Lord. Let me see today, and each duty in this day, as you see it.

8

IF I BELITTLE...

*Consider what a great forest is set on fire by a
small spark. The tongue also is a fire....*

JAMES 3:5–6

*Jesus said ..., "Anyone who says [to his brother or
sister], 'You fool,' will be in danger of the fire...."*

MATTHEW 5:22

If, in any way, I belittle those who I am called to
serve ...

if I talk of their weak points in contrast, perhaps,
with what I think of as my stronger points ...

if I adopt a superior attitude, forgetting to consider
the wisdom of the voice that asks me, inwardly, "Who
made you different from the one you are criticizing—
and what do you have that you have not been *given?*"...

if I can easily discuss the shortcomings or the sins
of any man or woman ...

if I can speak in an off-handed way, even of a child's wrongdoing . . .

then I know nothing of Calvary love.

If: pp. 13–14

MY FATHER, HOW OFTEN do my words "singe" someone else? (And how much time do I spend thinking critically about another—so that nothing but words that singe come out?)

Today, Lord, work in *me*. Change the thought-life in me when I strip others of dignity . . . or reduce them point by point . . . in order to build myself up.

And give me your voice, to speak words of value . . . admiration . . . encouragement . . . compassion . . . true kindness. . . .

9

PERSONAL PREFERENCE
OVER LOVE

*Jesus said . . . "I will come to you. Before long the
world will not see me any more, but you will see me.
Because I live, you also will live. On that day, you will
realize that I am in the Father, and you
are in me, and I am in you. . . ."*

JOHN 14:18B–20

If I hold on to choices of any kind, just because they
are my choices . . .

if I give more room to my private likes and
dislikes . . .

if I am soft on myself and slide easily and comfort-
ably into the vice of self-pity and eliciting sympathy . . .

if I do not, by the grace of God, build a fortress
around my inner man to protect it from my own
soulishness . . .

if, the very moment I am conscious of the shadow
of "self" crossing that inner threshold, I do not shut
the door and (in the power of Him who works in us to

will and to do) keep that door *shut* . . .
  then I know nothing of Calvary love.

If: pp. 35, 37, 39

MY FATHER, SO OFTEN I merely *react* to what I see and hear. Then I feel so superficial. I wonder why my "Christianity" has so little power . . . seems so unlovely. Then I realize I have done it my own way, and I feel like I've stepped "outside" of you.

But today, I want my life—all thoughts, words, actions—to flow up and out of a spirit that lives "within" you.

Come meet with me now, Father, in the secret inner depths of my spirit!

10

SEEKING MEN'S PRAISE

The kingdom of heaven will be like . . .
a man going on a journey, who calls his servants
and entrusts his property to them. . . . After a long
time, the master of those servants returns
and settles accounts with them. . . .
"Well done, good and faithful servant!
You have been faithful in a few things,
I will put you in charge of many things.
Come and share your master's happiness!"

MATTHEW 25:1, 14, 19, 23

If the praise of others elates me . . .

if the blame of others depresses me . . .

if I cannot rest when I am misunderstood, without
defending myself . . .

if I love to be loved, more than to give love . . .

if I love to be served, more than serving . . .

then I know nothing of Calvary love.

IF: P. 59

> MY FATHER, SO SELDOM do I feel the rich and unshakable peace of heaven, which you promised to me. Is it because I am so often concerned with pleasing others—afraid they'll think poorly of me? Do I work too hard, as if it's my job, to make certain people happy?
>
> Am I living outside your kingdom of peace, Father, because I'm serving the wrong master?

11

ENTANGLEMENTS

You then ... be strong in the grace that is in Christ Jesus. ... No one serving as a soldier [entangles himself] in civilian affairs—he wants to please his commanding officer. ... Reflect on what I am saying, for the Lord will give you insight.

2 TIMOTHY 2:1, 4, 6

What is the ideal for one who is God's "emissary"?

He is to be *disentangled*.

The man or woman who would be God's emissary is a Nazirite, separated; a Priest, crowned. And along with these, a Soldier on service in a great campaign, one who cannot become entangled and caught in the "little affairs" of this life (as the Greek puts it). For our daily affairs are truly so little, as compared with the great affairs of the War we are all called to wage.

Unfortunately, the word "disentangled" cuts straight across much that is acceptable and even desirable to those of us who are the Lord's soldiers.

There is the social entanglement—even the things that are expected of us. How can we do what is required of us, say, by family and friends and service to community, and at the same time get the *quiet* we know we must have if we are to go on in strength and calmness of spirit?

There are daytime functions that, to a conscientious worker, often result in a crush—if the countless other things that need to be done (but are missed if they are not done) are to be peacefully accomplished. And there is the business of keeping late hours. Simple enough for those whose responsibilities do not call them up at dawn. But for those who, to have any sort of undisturbed quiet, must not only be up by dawn but "awaken the dawn" with their praise, late nights are quite another matter.

"It was so late when I got home," said one man, speaking of these so-called social duties, "that I'm too tired to read or to have an effective quiet time."

Quiet time. The term is vital, descriptive of the very manner in which we receive an in-flooding of the Lord's life. . . .

And there is a closely related entanglement: overwork. Who has not come under the weight of this one? The more we love our work, the keener we are to do it well. . . . But there is another aspect of this—and I would not even touch on it, except that it is so terribly common and so deadly in its entangling. I am referring to the perhaps unrealized ambition that drives us to work so hard—a love for the praise of men, which is not just an entanglement, but a deadly snare.

To those who are entangled in the ways I have described, there will always come a need to exercise the special energy that comes from a life lived in close union with the Lord. It may be a trial, from which our flesh shrinks in dismay. We may sense a coming conflict—the air itself, thick with good and evil forces, wrestling, and the evil so terribly strong. And yet we feel bound by invisible cords, and we ask "Why do I feel so weighted down, so hindered?"

In such a moment, we may call upon the God of fire to burn our bonds and set us free to fight the fight, to make us strong to stand, peaceful and strong, in heavenly places with Christ Jesus.

But we fail.

Is it because the Lord has moved farther from us than He used to be?

The heart breaks with the thought: *If only I had spent more time with God . . . I would have had more power. . . .*

The powers of darkness are as strong as ever. Times have not changed since the days when the Apostle Paul wrote: "For our struggle is not against flesh and blood. . . ." (Ephesians 6:12). Our fight with the spirits of evil is just as desperate now as it was then. The conditions of battle are still the same: "This kind does not go out but by prayer and fasting" (Matthew 17:21).

We cannot allow ourselves to be entangled and, at the same time, believe that we will have spiritual power.

GOD'S MISSIONARY: P. 3

MY FATHER, YOU ARE the One who rescues me from all the "snares" that are set by the great Enemy of my soul. I do praise you!

Open my eyes, Father, to the entanglements I've stumbled into!

Give me godly understanding . . . and let your powerful grace show the way of escape.

12

"TRIVIAL" PROFANITIES

*Jesus . . . cried in a loud voice, "If any man is thirsty,
let him come to me and drink! He who believes in
me—who cleaves to and trusts in and relies on me—
as the Scripture has said, 'Out from his innermost
being springs of living water shall continuously flow.'"*

JOHN 7:37–38, AMPLIFIED

What does it mean to say, God's true emissary is a
"Nazirite"?

A Nazirite was one who made a special vow—the
vow of one who is willing to be separated from worldly
pursuits and snares— to separate himself totally so he
may be put to service by the Lord. The special vow
meant total abstinence, even from certain things which
were not wrong in themselves and which, to other people, might actually be beneficial.

"As long as he is a Nazirite, he must not eat anything that comes from the grapevine, not even the
seeds or the skins" (Numbers 6:4).

Not even the seeds or the skins?

How often have we, as Christians, heard other Christians ask—in reference to certain books, or pursuits, or recreations—"What's the harm in it?" And really the question is, "What's the harm in it—even if it is unprofitable?"

"Surely there is no harm in recreation?" I have often heard this question asked, in a tone of reproach or surprise or disgust, depending on the frame of mind of the questioner.

To this, I must answer: "No, there is no harm in recreation—if by that you mean *a pastime that will re-equip you for future work, and will not cause a leakage of spiritual power.*" We must have a fresh in-flooding of life for soul and body too, or we will dry up and be like deserts in a desert.

The real question, however, is this: Where are we to find our fresh springs of life?

"Glorious things are said of you, O city of God. . . . All my springs [of joy] are in you!" (Psalm 87:3, 7).

Can you or I say the same thing, truthfully? Or is it not a fact that, quite without our realizing it, certain forms of "recreation" have taken hold of us and hinder rather than help?

On this point, I must remember that I am not dealing with the question of what is right or wrong for another—*any* other—but whether, as God's emissary, I have something to learn from the special vow of separation taken by the Nazirites. The essence of that vow, remember, is to abstain from things that, in themselves, were lawful and permissible but were not expedient. Even *raisins* were contraband. Surely there is no harm in raisins!

Those of us who are God's emissaries are to treat the world (not just its corruptions, but its legitimate joys, its privileges and blessings also), as a thing to be touched at a distance. We must be aware at all times that, if we are caught by its spirit, or fed by its meat, we will lose our sensitivity to the very breath of the Highest and will no longer receive the manna that falls from heaven to feed our souls.

It is not that He forbids us this or that indulgence or comfort; not that He is stern, calling us to a life of harsh asceticism, as if that would make Him more pleased with us. No, it is that we who love our Lord, and we whose affections are set on the things that are heaven for us *today*, will voluntarily and gladly lay aside things that charm the world, so that we may be charmed and ravished with the things of heaven. Then our whole being may be poured forth in constant and unreserved devotion in serving our Lord, who died to save us.

Therefore, we may bind ourselves to God with the kind of vow that commits us to this: to look upon the world, in all its delights and attractions, suspecting that traps are set there for us, reserving ourselves for a higher way. *The world is not for us.*

We are called to live daily in a higher Kingdom, where we are touched and our souls drink from the Spirit of God.

GOD'S MISSIONARY: PP. 4–5

MY FATHER, SO OFTEN I feel restless. Unsatisfied. Wanting something more. I try to satisfy my inner thirst for life in ways that don't satisfy—that only leave me thirstier still.

Maybe underneath, I don't really *believe* you are what you say you are: *Life itself, pure-flowing.*

Today, Father, help me to "cleave" to you—to embrace you fully with my trust. To see the things that draw me for the mirage they are. And to drink more deeply from your spring of living water.

13

INFECTIOUS FEAR

If God is for us, who can be against us? . . .

*. . . I am convinced that neither death nor life,
neither angels nor demons, neither the present nor the
future, nor any powers, neither height nor depth, nor
anything else in all creation, will be able to separate us
from the love of God that is in Christ Jesus our Lord.*

ROMANS 8:31, 37–39

Have you ever thought how infectious fear can be? It
spreads from one person to another more quickly and
certainly than any of the fevers we know so well.

You can refuse the spirit of fear, which never comes
to us from God. (And if He does not send it to us, who
does?) Instead, open your heart wide to the Spirit of
"power and love and a *calm* and *well-balanced* mind, and
discipline and *self-control*" (2 Timothy 1:7, Amplified).
Because fear is so infectious, let us, for the sake of others and ourselves, refuse it.

Thank God courage is as "infectious" as *dis*courage-ment. Haven't you often felt the cheer and strength that seem to flow from a person whose mind is fixed and firm on God? I have.

And I have been thinking of another, a *greater*, reason for refusing the spirit of fear.

When we are downhearted or fearful or weak, we are saying to everybody (by the way we look and by our timidity, if not by our words), "After all, the Lord can't be absolutely trusted."

Somewhere near us, though we do not see them, are others: Men and women who we can see; and also good angels and evil spirits who we cannot see. To all of these, when we give in to fear, we say the same dishonoring thing.

We have a Savior who has never once failed us. He never will fail us. He has loved and led and guarded us all these years.

Look to Him now and pray from the barren bedrock of your heart, if that is the "ground" you are standing on, "Lord, give me courage!"

EDGES OF HIS WAYS: P. 148

MY FATHER, I HAVE this *habit of fear*.

Sometimes I let my fear "exempt" me from doing what you have asked me to do:

"Speak My word to this one." ("But Lord, I'm afraid he'll think . . .")

"Contribute to this effort." ("But what if I won't have enough?")

Help me to cross the battle-line of fear that is drawn across the ground of my soul. You are *for* me, and nothing can stand against me!

14

JUST HIS TOUCH . . .

As many as touched him were made whole.

Many of us try to have a regular quiet time. As we do so, may each of us touch at least the hem of His garment and receive wholeness in the matter for which we seek Him (Matthew 9:20).

One knows when this has occurred. It is a day when something happens that is different from just reading our Bible or devotional book, or even just praying and asking for the thing.

We touch Him, and all is changed.

What happens? And who can tell *how* it happens?

We only know that something has passed from Him to us. For example:

- Courage to do the difficult task we feared.
- Patience to bear with that one particular trying person.

- Inner strength to go on when we were sure we could not.
- A sweet freshness in our spirit, complete inner happiness, deep-flowing peace.

God's way of passing by, of letting His "hem" come near us, is to take some single word in His Book and make it breathe spirit and life to us. Then, relying upon that word—meditating, feeding our soul on it—we find it is suddenly possible to go from strength to strength.

True, there is always some new, even daily challenge in our lives which calls for revitalized faith. And we can choose to go on with God. But He always passes by. There is always the word waiting in His Book, which will meet us where we are and carry us further on. True, it will be a fight to the end—Paul calls it "the good fight of faith" (1 Timothy 6:12). But full provision is made for victory in that fight.

And so, whether the struggle that engages us has to do with our inner life or our outward circumstances, there is nothing to fear. "For your Father has been pleased to give you the kingdom" (Luke 12:32).

We need never, and by His grace we *shall* never, be defeated.

THOU GIVEST—THEY GATHER: PP. 4–5

MY FATHER, I BELIEVE I see it now. I always want you to do something *for* me. (Or at least to clear the way, so I can do it for myself.) And you want to do something *in* me.

Now I see that you want to come with your word and your powerful Spirit, and splice them together with my words and my spirit.

I have wanted answers. You want us to become one. . . . Thank you, for your unending patience with me.

15

HE ALLOWS ME TO HUNGER

O God, you are my God, earnestly I seek you; my soul thirsts for you, my body longs for you, in a dry and weary land where there is no water. . . .
My soul will be satisfied as with the richest of foods; with singing lips my mouth will praise you.

PSALM 63:1, 5

The son found himself in a barren place.

His Father said, "In *this* place I will give you the peace you are longing for. *Here* I will give you spiritual food that will nourish you. You are always with Me—no matter what the circumstances—and all that I have is yours."

Then the Father, with great gentleness, drew the son to himself. Quietly He said, "I am the one who allowed you to come into these humbling circumstances and who allowed you to hunger. I did this so that I might feed you with *manna*—My bread from heaven!

"Only in this way could I help you to know that you cannot live by bread alone, but by every word that proceeds from My mouth."

The son said, "Give me this bread always!"

And when he grew thirsty he learned to cry, "The light of your face is my life!"

Later still, the son wondered why one like himself, who was so richly fed and cared for at times, should at other times feel so poor and needy and thirsty.

His Father replied by asking four questions:

"Can someone who has never thirsted know how precious is My living water?

"Can someone who has never discovered rivers of these living waters flowing on barren heights—can he ever lead his thirsty friend to those rivers?

"Can someone who has never walked the deep valleys of the spirit help a friend who is fainting—or lead this friend to the well-springs that will save the life of his soul?

"Can someone who has never seen burning sands in the wilderness turn into a refreshing pool—can he speak in praise of My marvels, or My power?"

HIS THOUGHTS SAID . . . HIS FATHER SAID: PP. 37–38

MY FATHER, I'VE BEEN struggling within because of some of the places life has led me . . . and struggling with you, too. . . .

I come to you today, Father, and ask you to begin refreshing and nourishing my soul again.

16

IF ONLY . . .

For this is what the high and lofty One says—he who lives forever, whose name is holy: "I live in a high and holy place, but also with him who is contrite and lowly in spirit, to revive the spirit . . . and to revive the heart . . ."

ISAIAH 57:15

In a letter written by Samuel Rutherford, dated 1640, he speaks of how hard it is to be patient if we allow our thoughts to become stuck "down among the confused rollings and wheels of *second causes.*"

By this he means all the times we say, "If only I hadn't been in the wrong *place,*" or "If only I'd gone at a different *time.*" He means the subtle temptation to link together earthly causes-and-effects. To fight against this temptation, to escape the confused, grinding, second wheels of this "logic," Rutherford cries to us from across history: "Look up! Look to the master-motion and the *first* wheel!"

There was a day, for me—October 24—when I stood among three other happy people in Joyous City, outside the door of the house we'd rented for the missions work there—which we'd found locked. We wondered what we should do. The old man who had charge of the key was not there, and the key was not to be found.

We stood a long time in the swiftly gathering twilight, ready to turn contentedly toward home if we could not get in. Just then, another old man hurried up, the huge key of his own courtyard door in hand. "This may open it," he said hopefully.

There was a moment's fumbling. The door opened. We went in. . . .

What if the old man had not rushed up at the last moment with a key? What if the key had not worked? There was a pit dug, where no pit was supposed to be. And for me, a crippling fall.

The confused rollings and wheels of "second causes" do not help much here—or anywhere. The Lord allowed it. Therefore, so far as we are concerned, He did it: He, himself. And all that He does is good.

On October 6, eighteen days before, a member of our fellowship was at home in London. In a time of prayer, he was suddenly caused to feel that danger was threatening me. He prayed, not the easy prayer of the unconcerned, but the intense prayer of one greatly burdened. A sense of fear tried to overwhelm him, as of a terror by night. He continued on until peace came, and he knew that his prayer was heard.

Should we have said that prayer was *not* answered? It is a petty view of our Father's love and wisdom which demands or expects an answer according to our desires, apart from His wisdom.

We see hardly one inch of the narrow lane of time. To our God, eternity lies open as a meadow. It must seem strange to the heavenly people, who have reached the beautiful End, that you and I should ever question what Love allows to be, or that we ever call prayer "unanswered" when it is not what we expect.

Isn't *no* an answer?

Isn't *heaven* an answer?

ROSE FROM BRIER: PP. 149–150

MY FATHER, I CRIPPLE myself spiritually by going over and over the "what ifs." I never saw this as pride—as trying to take your place as Lord and Shepherd. . . . I confess you now as the Master of time and eternity.

Be my Shepherd today, leading me on this "low" road I'm traveling.

17

CLOUDS

The Lord reigns forever...

PSALM 9:7

... and the righteous stand firm forever...

PROVERBS 10:25

*... and the fruit of righteousness will be peace;
and the effect of righteousness will be quietness
and confidence forever.*

ISAIAH 32:17

This evening the clouds hung low on the mountains, so that sometimes we could hardly see the familiar peaks. Sometimes the stars, too, were nearly all covered. But always, just when it seemed as though the mountains were going to be quite lost in the mist, the higher peaks pushed out and, whereas the dimmer stars were veiled, the brighter ones shone through.

Even supposing the clouds had wholly covered the face of the mountains, and not a star shone through the piled-up masses, the mountains would *still* have stood steadfast and the stars would not have ceased to shine. I thought of this and found it very comforting, simple as it was.

Our feelings do not affect God's facts. They may blow up, like clouds, and cover the eternal things that we do most truly believe. We may not see the shining of the promises—but still they shine! And the strength of the hills that is His also, is not for one moment less because of our human weakness.

Heaven is no dream. Feelings go and come, like clouds. But the "hills" and "stars" abide.

EDGES OF HIS WAYS: MARCH 27

MY FATHER, I WILL anchor my *self,* my *thoughts* and my *will,* in these facts:

You *are.*

You rule in heaven and on the earth.

You call me "righteous" because I am in Jesus, your son.

No matter what it may seem, I will stand firm forever.

18

LOST, ALONE, ISOLATED

*In my distress I called to the Lord; I cried to my God
for help. From his temple he heard my voice. . . .
He parted the heavens and came down; dark
clouds were under his feet. . . . He made darkness his
covering, his canopy around him. . . . Out of the
brightness of his presence clouds advanced. . . . He shot
his arrows and scattered my enemies, great
bolts of lightning and routed them.*

PSALM 18:6, 9, 11–12, 14

There was one who was unafraid of any evil that might
rise against her, unafraid of even the hint of bad news.
Her heart stood fast, believing the Lord, trusting in the
tender mercy of God for ever and ever.

How often He had arisen as light in the darkness!
How often she had called upon Him from the very center of trouble, knowing that He heard her the instant
each storm broke upon her, knowing He would come
at once and deliver her. He had been so full of love, and
she had sung and proclaimed His goodness, saying,

"Who is like the Lord our God—who has His dwelling so high, yet humbles himself to take part in things that are far below Him in heaven and on earth?"

But now . . .

She found herself standing alone, isolated, looking into a great gray mist.

Fold after fold, the hills lay before her, but always in impenetrable mists. She could see no path. Only a little track in the valley below. She felt quite alone. For a while she stood. Listening. Feeling an inward isolation and uncertainty harder to bear than any acute physical pain had ever been.

Softly, voices began to speak within her. Now stealing her courage, now filling her with courage again:

"My heart and my flesh fail. . . ."

"But God is the strength of my heart, and the good portion that is allotted to me—forever!"

"My closest friends avoid me, or else they have no idea what is happening in the depths of my soul. And even my own family does not understand. . . ."

"Nevertheless, I am with you moment by moment, because you have reached out for my strong hand."

"My tears have flowed day and night, while unbelievers look at me and think, *Where is your God now?*"

"You shall answer for me, 'The Lord is God!' "

"Why are you cast down, O my soul—and why are you so unsettled within me?"

"Hope in Me, your God! For you shall yet praise Him, who gives the very blush of health to your face."

"No, the path I'm forced to walk is hidden from God. . . ."

I know the ways that you must walk. All your ways are before me. As for Me, my way is perfect and I make your way perfect. The people never thirsted even when I led them through the desert. Will you faint, though I lead you through mist-clouded hills?"

When her inner struggle ceased, she looked again at the mist—and saw that a great light was growing in its very heart. At once, she knew that she was not alone, had never been alone. God *was* her refuge and strength, present with her, ready to help in times of trouble! (Psalm 46:1).

Suddenly, He was all about her path. He would make good on His promises of lovingkindness toward her, and He comforted her. He would not let any of her hopes be disappointed. Nor could she fear any longer, for those gloomy paths that lay ahead, through the folds of the hills, they were open ways to Him.

So it was enough for her to see only the next few steps. He would go before her and make His own footsteps a way for her to walk in! She was filled again with assurance: The One whom she followed could see through the mist all the way to the end of the path.

And as she walked the misted way, she was given a song to sing: "You, my Lord, never fail those who seek you!"

As she walked and sang, others whom she did not see because the mist lay heavy all about her, heard her singing.

And though she did not know it, she gave many comfort and helped them to follow in the path of His footsteps too—all the way to end.

FIGURES OF THE TRUE: P. 3

MY FATHER, IS THE mist around me really the advancing edge of your powerful storm, to drive away my enemies?

I know that you hear my voice when I call for help. Give me courage to stand, through all gathering darkness, so that I can encourage others when your brightness is at last revealed.

19

WHEN I CALL, YOU HEAR!

I will praise you, O Lord, with all my heart. Before the "gods" I will sing your praise. . . . When I called, you answered me; you made me bold and stouthearted.

PSALM 138:1, 3

Some find it hard to believe that Satan—a conquered foe—can interfere in the affairs of a child of God.

Yet we read about the Apostle Paul, working earnestly and with all his might in something the Lord has given him to do, and Satan hinders him. The reason for Satan's power to interfere in Paul's life was *not* prayerlessness. As he wrote to the Christians in Thessalonica, whom he eagerly wanted to reach, "Night and day [I] pray most earnestly that [I] may see you again and supply what is lacking in your faith" (1 Thessalonians 3:10).

We see that Satan could not touch Paul's *spirit*, or any other vital thing in him. But he could so order events that the apostle could not do, for these children of his love, all that he longed to do. He could only write letters. He could not be with them.

In another passage, we see a thing in Paul's life that is stranger still: "To keep me from becoming conceited . . . there was given me a thorn in my flesh, a messenger of Satan, to torment me" (2 Corinthians 12:7). A messenger of Satan, allowed to do bodily hurt—and we are not told for how long.

From this we understand that there are activities in the unseen world which are not explained to us. Every now and then the curtain between is drawn aside for a moment, and we see. But it is soon drawn back again. So much we do not know.

But this we *do* know: "When I call, you answer! You give me strength." If that is true, what does any present trouble matter?

How I wish to be able, in my life, to turn all disappointments, setbacks, and trials of faith and patience the way Paul used his! What reward, what golden treasure came to our Lord because Paul endured and was victorious in his difficult circumstances.

Even though Paul had so much to endure—not only physical hardships but loneliness and very human longings—look at the way he closed his first letter to the Thessalonians:

May God himself, the God of peace, sanctify you through and through. May your whole spirit, soul and body be kept blameless at the coming of our Lord

Jesus Christ. The one who calls you is faithful and he will do it (1 Thessalonians 5:24–25).

He *will* do all that I long to do, and cannot. *Faithful is He: He will do it!*

EDGES OF HIS WAYS: PP. 141–142

MY FATHER, I SEE that Paul had within him the potential to be conceited—a hidden kingdom of pride.

Are there hidden kingdoms within me that you are trying to break into, so you can rescue me from myself?

Are my present struggles, which feel like the pounding of a battering ram, only your gentle but persistent knock at my heart-gate?

20

LOOK UP TO HIM . . .

*He who began a good work in you will carry it on
to completion until the day of Christ Jesus. . . .
Continue to work out your salvation. . . .
For it is God who works in you to will
and to act according to his good purpose.*

PHILIPPIANS 1:6; 2:12–13

There are countless promises given to us by the Lord
for times when things are hard. There is one in the Old
Testament, which was given first to Moses, then to
Joshua: "I will never leave you or forsake you" (Deuteronomy 31:6; Joshua 1:5).

Lest we should fear that it was spoken only or
specially to Joshua, the writer of a New Testament book
quotes it just as if it were spoken to him and to all of
us who read his book: " 'I will never leave you or forsake you.' So we may say with confidence, 'The Lord is
my helper' " (Psalm 118:6–7).

I like that part, "*with confidence*," don't you?

We are not meant to shake with fear when faced by temptations. We may look up to Him who conquered the powers of evil when He "reigned from the Tree" (Psalm 96:10, Jerome).

Those powers can never say that He did not conquer them, for He both exposed them and made a show of conquering them openly.

Therefore, we follow in procession behind a triumphant Christ! And if all our reliance is placed upon Him, we need never be defeated in spirit. Today, from hour to hour, He *can* and *will* lead us on to triumph— if we look to Him.

And if some duty or service has to be done which seems quite impossible, the same promise of help and triumph holds true. Over and over again I have seen the Lord do "impossible" things. I think He delights in the impossible!

And He delights to meet the faith of one who looks up to Him and says, "Lord, you know that I cannot do this—but I believe that *you* can!"

EDGES OF HIS WAYS: PP. 147–148

My Father, so often, I rely on myself to be strong enough, good enough—still thinking that I have to make myself presentable and worthy of your love.

Help me, today, to cease from all my inner striving . . . to rest in you . . . knowing that you will see me through every temptation to be like the old *me* and not like *you*. . . .

21

EVEN THIS...

*Who is this? He commands even the winds
and the water, and they obey him?*

LUKE 8:25

Even.

Is there something you are facing—whether in your outer circumstances or in your inner character—that seems impossible to command? Something that has baffled you and outwitted you a thousand times, and appears that it will win over you in the end? Something as deaf to your command as the wind or wild waters?

Don't despair. Don't shrug and give up.

Our Lord—your Lord and mine—can command even the most difficult, unruly thing that seems as if it will never be commanded.

Let His word "even" be a comfort to you. He who commands even the winds and water (and they *must* obey Him)—*He* can say to that "even" of yours, "Peace, be still."

And there will come for you "a great calm" (Mark 4:39).

Remember that there is nothing you are asked to do in your own strength. Not the least thing, nor the greatest:

God, who is all the while supplying the impulse [to obey and to overcome], giving you the power of inner resolve [to see it through to victory], is also giving you the strength to perform [under pressure] and to carry out His good pleasure. (Philippians 2:13 WAY'S TRANSLATION)

All the tremendous forces of nature—weather and politics and human nature too—are at the beck and call of our God. Each has only a faint shadow of the spiritual power that is His, and that He is ready to send forth for us.

Isn't that amazing?

How utterly foolish it is to plead weakness when we—even you and I—may move into the stream of that power. *If only we will....*

THOU GIVEST—THEY GATHER: PP. 19–20

MY FATHER, I CHOOSE your strength over my weakness!
   For today, I will step out of the role of Lord and Judge ... and I'll strike the word "impossible" from my thoughts!

22

THE MUSIC OF HIS
LOVINGKINDNESS

*Do not say in your heart,
"Who shall ascend into heaven?" (that is,
as if we need to bring Christ down to us).*

ROMANS 10:6

*God raised us up with Christ, and seated us with him
in the heavenly realms in Christ Jesus.*

EPHESIANS 2:6

No Christian man or woman was ever meant to walk on the natural plane. There is no provision made for such a walk. Always, God's promise is that His child will break through and live and endure as if he were seeing only the workings of the invisible world, not fixed on physical senses.

God himself made full provision for us to live this way: "My grace is more than enough . . ." (2 Corinthians 12:9).

As you take in those words, you will find yourself compassed about with songs. As one who walks in a garden or in a green woods at sunrise, hearing on all sides little snatches of song, so it will be with you . . . a music will flow over the inward ear. . . .

It is another kind of music, though, not heard in this world. The singers are as unseen as the morning birds among the green leaves. And yet, like the birds, they are our dear companions: They are the heavenly people of the cloud of witnesses who surround us all about.

In this way, the Lord commands to us His loving-kindness: Above and beneath, behind and before us, it flows like broad rivers and streams. . . . The ships of the enemy cannot sail those waters. It is a forbidden thing.

Do not be afraid in the least, therefore, even if you are facing some inescapable trial or testing in this world. "The Lord your God will carry you, as a father carries his son, all the way . . ." (Deuteronomy 1:31).

GOLD BY MOONLIGHT: PP. 22–23

MY FATHER, CLOSER to me than my own heartbeat . . . more urgent to my life than the air I'm breathing. . . .

Thank you, Father, that you allow nothing to keep us apart today!

23

A CHANCE TO DIE . . .

I have been crucified with Christ and I no longer live,
but Christ lives in me. The life I live in my body,
I live by faith in the Son of God, who
loved me and gave himself for me.

GALATIANS 2:20–21

The words of our Lord are often swords, quick and powerful, and sharper than any two-edged blade.

And sometimes they are pearls—or even like tiny seed pearls, easily overlooked. But how beautiful when they are found! His words about we who are called to be His lights in this world, are precious seed pearls:

Neither do men light a candle and put it under a
bushel, but on a candlestick; and it giveth light to all
that are in the house. Let your light so shine before all
men. . . . (Matthew 5:15-16, KJV)

The candlelight will even shine through the windows

on the people who pass by in the street outside. In one of the Indian hospitals, there was at one time just such a "candle". . . .

One day, in this woman's hearing, something was said to a younger helper which almost drew from her a flashing, angry remark. But at that moment, a word was spoken to her inwardly: "*See in this, a chance to die.*"

And though spoken inwardly, it was far more clearly heard than many a word addressed to the outward ear.

"*See in this*"—this provoking, this rebuke that should not have been—"*a chance to die.*" To self, and the pride that comes from defending self.

"*See in anything*"—anything that rouses you to claim your "rights," or even to consider them at all—"*a chance to die.*"

Welcome anything that calls you to your only true position: "I have been crucified with Christ . . ." (Galatians 2:20).

A crucified life cannot be self-assertive. It cannot protect itself. It cannot be startled into resentful words. The cup that is full of sweet water cannot spill bitter-tasting drops, however sharply it is knocked.

GOLD BY MOONLIGHT: PP. 80–81

MY FATHER, ON FIRST look, these are difficult words: "crucified with Christ."

On second look, I see the promise . . . that you can so free me from the soul that is yet immature . . . unsettled . . . demanding. . . .

I see that you want me to pass beyond "crucified," to share in your risen brightness.

24

JOY IS NOT "GUSH"

*The ransomed of the Lord will enter ... with singing;
everlasting joy will crown their heads ...
and sorrow and sighing will flee away.*

ISAIAH 51:11–12

*Jesus said, "Now is your time of grief, but I will
see you again and you will rejoice, and
no one will take away your joy."*

JOHN 16:22

Thunderclouds are nothing to the Spirit of Joy. The only special reference to the joy of the Holy Spirit is bound up with the words "severe suffering":

... in spite of severe suffering, you welcomed the message [of fellowship with Jesus Christ] with the joy given by the Holy Spirit. (1 Thessalonians 1:6b)

Joy is not *gush*.
Joy is not mere *jolliness*.

Joy is perfect acquiescence—acceptance, rest—in God's will, whatever comes. And that is so only for the soul who delights himself in God.

Jesus, our Lord, took God as His *God* as well as His *Father*, and that brought Him to say His delight was "to do the will of Him who sent me" (John 6:38)—even though that meant the cross and such agony as no man has ever known. To do the will of God cost Him blood.

It cost Him blood.

Accept for yourself the Fatherhood of God, which is only possible for you and me because of the sacrifice of the blessed Son our Savior. And by the presence of the Holy Spirit within, you will learn to rejoice in the will of God, and nothing else.

This, then, is the call to the soul that would ascend above all earthly circumstance, to walk in heavenly places: Leave yourself open to the circumstances of His choice, for that is perfect acceptance, and rest in the will of God.

If you do so, you are not a fool—you are in the company of the brave!

For accepting the will of God in this way, "You became imitators of us," Paul writes, "and of the Lord" (1 Thessalonians 1:6a).

Are you following in their path?

GOLD BY MOONLIGHT: PP. 74–75

MY FATHER, WITH THE lifeblood of Jesus . . . you bought joy *for* me . . . and strength in the day of trouble. . . .

Thank you for sending so many others to walk the path of faith ahead of me. . . . I will keep seeking you . . . following you!

25

REPUTATION

Let this mind be in you which was also in Christ Jesus:
Who ... made himself of no reputation.

PHILIPPIANS 2:5–7, KJV

Years ago, I was staying with some friends in Scotland, near the place where a convention was being held in a big barn. Many speakers were there who had been touched with the fire of God at the great Keswick revivals, and some were staying in the house where I stayed.

We had our meals together in a large dining room, around one long table. I was the youngest one present.

One morning at breakfast, one of the speakers suddenly looked straight across the table at me. And slipping *my name* into the song, he began to sing very loudly to the tune "What a Friend We Have in Jesus"—only he began with these words:

Have you lost your reputation?
Are you trusting in the Lord?

The whole tableful of people stopped talking instantly and turned their full attention. In the horror of that moment, I missed the next two lines, but the man singing went on ruthlessly, still fixing me with the steady stare of his great blue eyes:

Have you found a full salvation
    from what people think and say?
Do you mean to live for Jesus,
    let the world say what it may?

By this time the others at the table, in pity, interrupted the song.

It took a long while to recover my peace.

But the words were unforgettable. I have lived to thank God for them—though I cannot imagine a more appalling way to convey spiritual truth!

Have you lost your reputation?

To lose it—and to keep on being willing to lose it daily for His sake and for the sake of those for whom He died—means this: To take up your cross daily (Luke 9:23).

There is one way of losing your reputation that is likely to come to you if you love your Lord enough and if you love other people enough. You will need to learn to refuse to give sympathy when it is asked for—because sympathy weakens another soul. Smooth sayings never helped a soul.

Say that someone comes to you full of complaints about how hard things are. They want pity. They want you, in fact, to say what Satan said through Peter to our Lord: "Oh no! God will never let anything hurtful come to you." (See Matthew 16:22.)

We may meet this desire for sympathy in a way that sends the other man or woman away happy, in a kind of sloppy happiness. We are happy to hear people say of us, "How well she understands me," or "I knew he would understand."

Or we may respond on another line: "Consider it pure joy . . . when you face trials of any kind . . ." (James 1:2).

But we hesitate to do this. And why?

Because we fear that something very different may be said about us when we are not around. And we fear that this person will no longer seek us out for friendship and "counsel," but will find "more sympathetic" friends. (A weak soul knows where to find more weakness!)

We fear, beneath it all, that we will lose every shred of our reputation for "love" and "understanding."

In point of fact, it may take a long time to lead that friend out of pity and into victory. And that is where the daily "walk" comes for you and me—when that friend rejects us, as He was rejected (Isaiah 53:3).

Will you accept this kind of rejection, for His sake?

It is hard, and we hesitate. But in the end, the choice is clear—which is dearer: your reputation, or the soul for whom He died?

THOU GIVEST—THEY GATHER: PP. 135–136

MY FATHER, I RESIST the thought of rejection. Until I see through my fear to the *promise* . . . a new *possibility*. . . .

If I am only *willing* . . . I can find at work in me a new love for others . . . a new mind . . . the truly compassionate mind of my Lord and brother . . . Jesus. . . .

26

EYES TO SEE

How great is his goodness,
and how great is his beauty!

ZECHARIAH 9:17, KJV

Just now I have been seeing something of the beauty of God in His lovely flowers. "But the Lord of beauty is more beautiful still, for He has created the flowers" (Wisdom 13:3).

In one of the apocryphal books it is written: "Go your way, and see beauty and greatness ... as much as your eyes are able to see" (2 Esdras 10:55). The one speaking was referring to the beauty of the great walls, palaces and temple courts of Jerusalem—but the words come to me often, with deeper meaning.

As much as your eyes are able to see.

How much are our eyes able to see of our Lord Jesus?

I have watched people looking through a microscope. Some glance for a moment, then shrug and move away. They have seen nothing. Others look for two or three seconds and say, "How amazing," or "How beautiful." They too move away, having seen more—but not much more.

It is only as we look and look and look that we really see. And the more we know of the object we are looking at, the more we see *in* it.

Paul speaks of "... the surpassing greatness of knowing Christ Jesus my Lord, for whose sake I have lost all things" (Philippians 3:8). He was willing to lose all things and to keep looking and looking and looking into Christ so that he might know Him better.

How much are we willing to lose, that we may know, and so be able to see?

It is the *I* in you and me that blinds our eyes. The loss of *I*—that I may know Him, see Him with new clearness in all creation ... even in souls that are unlovable and unbeautiful. May the Lord grant this to us all.

I want more and more to see His goodness and His beauty. Not vaguely, nor just from time to time. I want to see Him truly, continually, in His work, in those who love Him, in His Book, in *himself*.

THOU GIVEST—THEY GATHER: PP. 161–162

MY FATHER, THIS MOMENT, I push aside all sense of
need . . . every request . . . each complaint . . . even words
of praise or worship . . .

. . . just to stand silent . . . to turn the eyes of my soul
to you . . . to look deep into your wonders. . . .

27

POWERS ARRAYED
AGAINST ME

For our struggle is not against flesh and blood, but against the rulers, against the authorities, against the powers of this dark world and against the spiritual forces of evil in the heavenly realms.

EPHESIANS 6:12

. . . even the archangel Michael, when he was disputing with [Satan] over the body of Moses, did not dare to bring a slanderous accusation against him, but said, "The Lord rebuke you!"

JUDE 9

His anxious thoughts said: "Terrific powers are set in array against me!"

His Father said: "And you are as a little child, who knows not how to meet them. But with you, there is one stronger than they. *Do not forget to sing!*"

When the Israelites began to sing and praise, the Lord set ambushes for their enemy, Amalek. Because the hand of Amalek was turned, not against the

Israelites whom they attacked in the wilderness, but against the throne of God, the Lord declared war on them from generation to generation (1 Samuel 15:2–3).

Therefore, do not be afraid and do not be discouraged, though a great crowd is set against you. For the Lord your God, He shall fight against them together with you—with powerful effect!

HIS THOUGHTS SAID . . . HIS FATHER SAID: P. 60

MY FATHER, NOTHING I can do to defend myself is greater than you and the mighty wall of love and protection you have raised around me!

Today, though the Accuser comes . . . though I accuse myself . . . I will rest, instead, in you . . . my True Defense.

28

YOUR JOY

If you remain in me and my words remain in you,
ask whatever you wish and it will be given to you. . . .
I have told you this, so that my joy may be in you
and that your joy may be complete.

JOHN 15:7, 11

Your joy.

A strange "word" to come from God, considering the circumstance, but it was the first that came to me.

I had never thought I would be confined to a bed all day long. I expected always to be strengthened, so that I could either ignore or tread under foot bodily illnesses, and (having earnestly prayed for this) to pass straight from the midst of problems without giving anyone a moment's trouble.

What has happened, then, is strange to my nature. The shining happiness I experienced, through months when my will-power could do nothing to conquer pain (and it could not simply be ignored), was not natural.

It was one of those surprises from our heavenly Lover, who never tires of giving us surprises.

The "word" came to me the morning after the accident. I experienced a terrible fall in the little Indian town called Joyous City, where some of us had gone to prepare for the two missionaries from our group who were about to move there. This fall broke a bone, dislocated an ankle, and caused other internal hurts much harder to heal.

We made the difficult night drive of forty-six miles back home to our mission base and, by the time we arrived, the effects of the merciful pain-killer were beginning to wear off. It was then, as if through a haze, I heard our chief nurse saying something about wishing to take the pain from me—and I knew she meant that she wanted to bear the pain herself, in my stead.

That was when I heard myself spontaneously answer, *"Your joy, no one takes away...."*

It was like echoing aloud something heard deep within me. I did not recognize it as a Scripture verse, only that it was a certain and heavenly word given to me—truly a word of peace, even exultation! I could see our whole great missionary "family," each one wanting to bear the pain for me. Yet because of the intense comfort of that word, I was glad and grateful that it was impossible for them to do so.

And now, so that you may know why I humbly venture to write to those who know so much more of the awful, trampling power of pain than I do, I will tell how it was that I thought to write about all I have learned.

One day, after many, many nights when, in spite of all that was done to induce sleep, it refused to come (except in brief snatches), I received a letter from a friend. It went on at some length, with what sounded almost like pleasure, about my "enforced rest," and the silly phrase rankled me like a thorn. I was far too exhausted to laugh it off, as one can laugh off things when one feels well.

So *this* was supposed to be rest? And was the Father breaking, crushing, "enforcing" by weight of sheer physical misery, a child who only longed to obey His slightest wish? These words—"enforced rest"—had what I now know was an absurd power to distress me. They held such an unkind, such a false conception of our Father.

Until the moment I'd read these words—although I was puzzled about my accident—I'd not had one unhappy minute or inner restlessness, and that was because I had been given peace in acceptance. The spirit *can* live above the flesh, and mine, helped by the tender love of our Lord Jesus and the dearness of those around me, had done so.

But the moment I read these words of "comfort," and for a long while after, it was different. I had no peace. Not till I heard deep within me soft and soothing words again, such as a mother uses: "Let not your heart be troubled. Don't you know that I understand what you are suffering? What do men's words matter to Me, or to you?"

And I knew once again that the Father understood His child, and the child her Father.

I will share my crumb of comfort: Do not be weighted down with "flying" words. Do not expect your peace to come from the mouths of men. And do not allow the ignorant stock phrases of the "well" to the "ill" to penetrate your shield. How can they, the unwounded, know anything about the matter?

But the Lord our Creator knows! And all who have suffered know: Pain and helplessness are not "rest" and never can be; nor is the weakness that follows acute pain; nor the tiredness that is so tired of being inwardly tired. These things are poles apart from true rest.

Our Father knows that our rest is found only in receiving a sense of *well-being*—a well-being that, no matter our circumstances, is like the sense one has after a gallop on horseback, or a plunge in a forest pool or the glorious sea. . . . *He knows it!* He created us so, and can the Creator ever forget? If He remembers what true rest is, what does it matter that others forget?

Thus, we can be comforted and filled with His gift, an inward sweetness. And we can thank Him even when others trample unawares upon us, talking smooth nothings.

Rose From Brier: p. 1

MY FATHER, YOU KNOW the things that weigh me down . . . hurtful words . . . crushing circumstances. . . .

I will be gracious when others offer "smooth nothings." I will listen only for your words, and let my spirit rest in the assurance that comes with your every whisper to me. . . .

29

WISHES THAT BECOME CLOUDS

Don't be deceived, my brothers. Every good and perfect gift is from above, coming down from the Father of the heavenly lights, who does not change like shifting shadows.

JAMES 1:16–17

For no matter how many promises God has made, they are "Yes" in Christ. And so, through him, the "Amen" is spoken by us, to the glory of God.

2 CORINTHIANS 1:20

I had asked the doctor how long it would be before I could get back to my work. He had said I must be in splints for eight weeks, and I had taken this to mean I would be *well* in eight weeks. (And even that much time seemed like eight *years* to look forward to.)

I never dreamt of what really lay ahead. . . .

For some days the pain was dulled; then it came on with a severity which was to increase for many weeks (and, in one form or another, for months). Then came a day when I was opened to a new and deeper experience of the Lord's presence with me.

It began when I read a heretofore not much noticed word, from Psalm 105:18. Speaking of Joseph, the psalmist writes, "[his] feet they hurt with fetters; he was laid in iron" (KJV). Curious, I looked up this verse in a Greek translation of the Old Testament, where a commentator rendered a different view of this Scripture: "Joseph's *soul* entered into iron—entered, whole and entire in its resolve to obey God, into the cruel torture."

My soul was not in "cruel torture," but my foot was badly hurt. And as I lay there, unable to move, it came to me that what was asked of Joseph, in a far greater degree, was asked of me now. Would I merely "endure it," praying for the grace not to make too much over my poor circumstances? Or would my soul willingly enter into the "iron" of this new and difficult experience?

There could only be one answer to that. And when, on the following Sunday evening, a word was given from Philippians 1:13—"My bonds in Christ"—I knew that all was well indeed.

So there could be nothing but peaceful acceptance. And when one accepts, then *all* that is included in the thing accepted is accepted too—in my case, the helplessness, the limitations, the disappointments of hope deferred, the suffering.

I now know this is important in keeping our own spiritual "atmosphere" clear. For if we let even the fugitive wisp of a cloud float across our sky (in the form of a wish—that is, a wish that things were different!), then the whole sweet blue of our spirit is swiftly overcast.

But if we refuse that wisp of cloud. . . . If we look up and meet the love of the Lord that shines down on us, and say to Him about that particular detail of the trial, "Dear Lord, *yes*. . . ."

Then in one bright moment, our sky is blue again.

ROSE FROM BRIER: P. 2

MY FATHER, I WILL say—no matter what shadows of circumstance blow across my way—you are my *Father of Lights*. Coming down from heaven are good and perfect gifts to me. . . .

All the promises of your love and goodness are still . . . *Yes!* and *Amen!*

30

COME FORTH AS GOLD

*Dear friends, now we are children of God, and what
we will be has not yet been made known. But we
know that when he appears we will be like him, for
we shall see him as he is. Everyone who has this
hope in him purifies himself, just as he is pure.*

1 JOHN 3:2–3

Through these months, *acceptance* has been a word of
liberty and victory and peace to me. But it has never
meant acquiescence in illness, as though evil circumstances were from Him who delights to deck His servants with health.

But it did mean contentment with the unexplained.

Neither Job nor Paul ever knew (so far as we know)
why prayer for relief was answered as it was—with long,
initial silence. But I think they must now stand in awe
and joy, as they meet others in the heavenly country
who were strengthened and comforted by their patience
and courage. They must stand in awe, too, as they

understand now the Father's thoughts of peace toward them.

Hardly a life goes deep but has tragedy somewhere in it. What would such people do without Job? And who could spare from the soul's hidden history the great words spoken to the Apostle Paul: "My grace is sufficient for you, for my power is made perfect in weakness" (2 Corinthians 12:9). Such words lead straight to a land where there is gold, and the gold of that land is good.

Gold—the word recalls Job's affirmation: "But he knows the way that I take; when he has tested me, I will come forth as gold" (Job 23:10). And it recalls the ringing words of the Apostle Peter: "[All kinds of trials come] so that your faith—of greater worth than gold, which perishes even though refined by fire—may be proved genuine" (1 Peter 1:7). And it brings the quiet words in Malachi: "He will sit as a refiner and purifier of silver . . ." (Malachi 3:3).

(I have often thanked God that the word there is not *gold*, but *silver*, an important shift, I think. Silver is of little account here in the Far East, and I often feel more like silver than gold.)

The picture of the Refiner is straight from Eastern life. The Eastern goldsmith sits on the floor by his crucible. For me, at least, it is not hard to know why the heavenly Refiner has to sit so long. The heart knows its own dross.

"How do you know how long to sit and wait? How

do you know when it is purified?" we asked our village goldsmith.

"When I can see my face in it," he replied.

Blessed be the love that never wearies, never gives up hope that, even in such poor metal our Father may at last see the reflection of His face.

ROSE FROM BRIER: P. 3

MY FATHER, IF YOU are working into me some traits I would not have chosen to work on myself (for example, patience!), then I ask for your grace to carry me through.

"Purify" me of everything but perfect *acceptance* in you. . . .

31

ALL MEANS ALL!

All the paths of the Lord are loving and faithful.
PSALM 25:10

All the paths . . .

I have pondered this verse lately, and have found that it feeds my spirit.

All does not mean "all—except the paths I am walking in now," or "nearly all—except this especially difficult and painful path." All must mean *all*.

So, your path with its unexplained sorrow or turmoil, and mine with its sharp flints and briers—and *both* our paths, with their unexplained perplexity, their sheer mystery—they are His paths, on which He will show himself loving and faithful. Nothing else; nothing less.

I am resting my heart on this word. It bears me up on eagle's wings. It gives courage and song and sweetness, too—that sweetness of spirit which is death to lose even for a half hour.

I remember in times past almost desperately repeating to myself these lines, written as though spoken from the lips of our Lord:

Am I not enough, My own—
    not enough for you?
Am I not enough, My own?
    I, forever and alone,
    I, *needing* you?

It was a long time before I could honestly answer, "Yes, you alone are enough for me." I remember the turmoil of soul I experienced before committing myself to follow Him on whatever path He would lead—remember as if it were yesterday. But at last—oh, the *rest* that came to me when I lifted my head and followed! For in acceptance there lies peace.

God bless you and utterly satisfy your heart . . . with *himself*.

CANDLES IN THE DARK: P. 46

MY FATHER, YOU ALONE . . . you *yourself* . . . are enough for me.

No matter what path you lead me on today, it is not strange and unknown to you. . . .

Only let me go with your presence!

32

REJECTION

*Why then is it written that the Son of Man
must suffer much and be rejected?*

MARK 9:12

Don't be surprised if *you* are rejected. It is part of learning the way of the cross. In his Gospel, Mark makes note of our Lord's own assertion that He "must suffer many things and" (as if this had to be mentioned especially) "be rejected."

You will find this statement truer every year as you go on, growing deeper in the Lord: If you and I follow the way He went, we will be rejected too.

Anything is easier. To be whipped would be easier.

Have you ever gone through your *New Testament*, marking the places where the iron of suffering, in one form or another, is mentioned? It's wonderfully enlightening. The book is full of joy, I know. But it is also full of pain, and the pain is taken for granted by our Lord and His closest friends.

As the Apostle Peter writes: "Do not be surprised at the painful trial you are suffering, as though something strange were happening to you" (1 Peter 4:12). And the Apostle James writes, concerning trials: "Consider it pure joy, my brothers . . ." (James 1:2).

But what if the suffering, the rejection, comes from those whom we love?

Wasn't our Lord's suffering caused by those He loved?

Oh, what a book the Bible is! If only we would steep our souls in its mighty comfort, we would never go far wrong—we would never lose heart. As Peter elsewhere assures us: "To this you were called, because Christ suffered for you, leaving you an example . . . you should follow in His steps" (1 Peter 2:21).

You and I are meant to follow in the steps of our Lord, not avoid them.

And you will find that the joy of the Lord comes as you go on in the way of the cross. It was a man who had nobody on earth to call his own true constant friend who said, "But even if I am being poured out like . . . an offering on the sacrifice and service coming from your faith, I am glad, and rejoice with all of you" (Philippians 2:17).

It is no small gift of His love, this opportunity to be offered up—something you would not naturally choose, something that asks for more than you would naturally give.

That's the proof of His love. So let joy grow within you when rejection comes—for you are offering to the

Lord what He asks you to offer Him: the chance to show you what He can do.

CANDLES IN THE DARK: P. 67

MY FATHER, TO BE rejected . . . to "offer it up" to you as a spiritual sacrifice. . . . Only you know fully how hard this is.

But I'm willing, Father . . . and you know how much I need the comfort of your love to bear my hurt . . . to help me make it through . . . until my spirit is "risen" again, in you. . . .

33

THE EVIL WHISPERER

Perseverance must finish its work. . . . For the sun
rises with scorching heat and withers the plant,
its blossom falls and its beauty is destroyed. . . .
Blessed is the man who perseveres under trial. . . .
Every good and perfect gift is from above, coming
down from the Father of lights, who does not
change like shifting shadows. He chose. . . .

JAMES 1:4, 11–12, 17–18, emphasis added

I am in the seventeenth month of my painful, wounded circumstances. But what are seventeen months?

"It is seventeen years since I sat up. . . ." So began a letter I received recently from a Christian woman in a London hospital.

I wonder if other people who are so burdened face what I face in myself. That even though their will has long ago been folded up in the blessed will of God, a strangely persistent *I* can rise up suddenly. I am startled to discover, so unexpectedly, "chaff" scattered upon the floor of what I had hoped was a clean-swept soul.

Isn't it good to know that, of His work *in* us (as is also true of His work *through* us while we are on this earth), there will come a day when He will say, "It is finished"? He will have winnowed all the chaff; only the good seed will remain; the *I* will be slain, never to come to life again; the soul will bloom as perfect as a flower. We shall be like Him then, for we shall see Him as He is! (1 John 3:2).

But what about *for now*? The heart that would grow in love for Him can have only one answer to that: "He chose our inheritance for us."

I remember with what delight I learned one day that the verb *to choose*, which is used in this psalm, is the same that is used to describe David choosing, out of all the possible stones in the brook, the five best suited for his purpose (1 Samuel 17:40). It occurred to me that our heavenly David, our "Beloved," chooses out of all possible circumstances—and they are *all* at His command—those best suited to fulfill His purpose for my life.

Yet the evil whisperer never forgets to come, whispering his appeal to that persistent *I*: "How good it would be to be free of these circumstances. When will that day come? How *long* it is in coming...." No, he never forgets to torment.

But I have found a definite and swift deliverance, in the very instant the whisperer comes, in turning to Him who is nearer than any whisperer. I say instantly, "Make pure the inmost desire of my heart."

Then there flows into me peace, and with it the

assurance of the Beloved. However things may *appear* to be, of all possible circumstances—those circumstances in whose midst I am set—these are the best that He could choose for me. We do not know how this is true—where would faith be if we did?—but we *do* know that all things that happen are full of shining seed.

Light is sown for us—not darkness.

ROSE FROM BRIER: P. 34

MY FATHER, I WILL settle it in my heart today. . . . You have chosen only *good* for me!

34

THE LIGHTS OF GLORY

[Says the Lord Almighty:] "But for you who revere my name, the sun of righteousness will rise with healing in its wings."

MALACHI 4:2

In the room where I am convalescing, a net curtain hangs over a door opposite to which my bed is set. In this hot weather, the door is usually open. The foot of my bed hides the lower portion of this curtain, but I can clearly see the upper part, and on a day when there is not much light on the other side, every fold in the curtain shows. But when the sun is shining on the trees outside, I can hardly see the net. It is there, but I can hardly see it for the glory of that light.

This small thing has continually been my "word" and my "vision."

The material, temporal, solid details of the physical limitations I have thought of as iron fetters remain. There is no removing or evading them. And my old way—of ignoring, or stepping over minor physical problems—is impossible now. My ability to accept what is happening to me hinges on this: I am acutely aware that there is another world, nearer than the physical world. Things temporal and solid here, are transparent in that air. Only there can one's spirit breathe and be strong.

Just recently a letter came from Switzerland, from a woman who had heard, apparently from a mutual friend to whom I'd written, about my curtain and its message to me. This woman wrote:

> My father was a manufacturer, and once he gave me lengths of black and white net. When my husband became a minister in a rural village, we had to protect ourselves against mosquitoes, so we put the white net on frames that fit over our windows. The result seemed excellent to us. When the light outside was poor, there was still only a dim haze between us and the outside—and on brighter days even this was lost.
>
> But in time, the white nets wore out. To our regret, we had only the black net to replace it. We could see through the black net clearly in every kind of light, so that we often hit our heads against it when we wanted to look out of the window, because we'd forgotten it altogether.
>
> That said to us: In the night the stars shine.

And beyond the cross, the love of God shines.
And all of our earthly sadness can be lost too, if
we hold it up before the light of Jesus.

. . . To all the children of the Father of Lights, however shadowed life may be, there is now, and there *will
be*, the Light that changes all things, and "makes all
things new" (Revelation 21:5).

And a light shined in the cell,
and there was not any wall,
and there was no dark at all!
Only you, Emmanuel.
Light of Love shined in the cell,
turned to gold the iron bars,
opened windows to the stars.
Peace stood there sentinel.
Dearest Lord, how can it be
that you are so kind to me?
Love is shining in my *cell*—
Jesus, my Emmanuel.

ROSE FROM BRIER: P. 6

MY FATHER, I CONFESS . . . sometimes I let myself become nothing more than a grumble in the darkness. . . .

But not today, Father!

Today, I await your "opened window to the stars."

I wait upon you, expecting that *this day* the Sun of Righteousness will rise with healing within me. . . .

35

THE BARE BUSH
IN SNOW . . .

*I know that the Lord is great . . . greater than all
gods. . . . He makes clouds rise from the ends of the
earth; he sends lightning with the rain and
brings out the wind from his storehouses.*

PSALM 135:5, 7

*"Have you entered [my] treasuries of snow . . .
which I reserve. . . ?"*

JOB 38:22–23

You were like a leafy bush, and many little things came
for you to shelter. You were not great or important, but
you could help those little things.

And it was the joy of your life to help them.

Now you can do nothing at all.

Some desolation—illness, monetary loss, or something you cannot talk about to anyone, a trouble no
one seems to understand—has overwhelmed you. All
your green leaves have gone.

Now you cannot shelter even the least little bird.

You are like a bush, with its bare twigs. No use to anyone.

That is what you think.

But look again at this bare bush. Look at the delicate tracery of its shadow lines on the snow. The sun is shining behind the bush and so every little twig is helping to make something that is very beautiful. Perhaps other eyes, that you do not see, are looking on it too, wondering what can be made of sun and snow and poor bare twigs. . . .

The spring will come again, for after winter there is always spring.

But when will the spring come? When will your bush be green with leaves again? When will the little birds you love come back to you? I do not know. Only I know that sun and snow are working together for good. And the day will come when the memory of helplessness and inability to give help to anyone else, or the memory of hard financial times, or of loneliness, loss or isolation—these will all pass as a dream in the night. All that seemed lost will be restored.

Now, in the midst of so much unhappiness, engulfing your heart in cold, let these words seep down—like fingers of sunlight, like trickles of first-spring rains—to refresh your inmost soul: He will not fail you, who is the God of the sun and the snow.

FIGURES OF THE TRUE: P. 1

MY FATHER, FORGIVE me for forgetting . . . that even when cold and snow come . . . you are still in charge of everything!

And you know, Father, that desolate place in me that needs the gentle touch of resurrecting rains today. . . .

36

A BARRIER AGAINST MY PURSUERS

Fight against them that fight against me.

PSALM 35:1

Block the way against those who pursue me.

PSALM 35:3

What are the things that fight against me?

Let us not lose the comfort and power that is available to us in this Scripture by relating the psalmist's prayer to the larger matters only. It touches on and includes the smallest, as well. The wave that sweeps over the great rock is the same that sweeps over the tiny shell on the shore.

It is the littlest things of life, the minute, unimportant-looking things, that are most likely to shatter our peace. Because they are so small, it is most likely that we will fight them ourselves instead of looking up at once to our Strong God—our Barrier between us and them, as the pillar of cloud formed a barricade between the Egyptians and Israel (Exodus 14:20).

"Fight against them that fight against me. . . ."

That is to say, against the little foolish feelings that want to keep us back from saying to the blessed will of God, "I am content to do whatever you say—fight against these pursuing feelings, O God!"

Then it will be true: "My soul will rejoice in the Lord and delight in his salvation. My whole being will exclaim, 'Who is like you, O Lord? You rescue the poor from those too strong for them'" (Psalm 35:9–10).

What joy our lives can be when we continually prove His tenderness in the very little things. There is nothing too small for Him to help. He is indeed a Barrier between us and our pursuers.

"How priceless is your unfailing love! Both high and low among men find refuge in the shadow of your wings!" (Psalm 36:7).

Now for a day of joy!

EDGES OF HIS WAYS: P. 137

MY FATHER, MAYBE I've been ashamed to admit it, but it's true. . . . It's those petty, little things that make me fail.

It's the moment's small distraction when I'm busy that brings out my impatience . . . the word that slights or insults that brings out my anger . . . all the small expenses that bring out my doubts about your ability to provide. . . .

I've let these enemies come inside my "barrier" . . . and raid my peace.

But today, Father, I come to hide myself again in you. . . .

37

TO BECOME HIS FLAMES
OF FIRE . . .

A veil covers [the hearts of the unbelieving]. But whenever anyone turns to the Lord, the veil is taken away. Now the Lord is the Spirit, and where the Spirit of the Lord is there is freedom. And we, who with unveiled faces all reflect the Lord's glory, are being transformed into his likeness with ever-increasing glory, which comes from the Lord who is the Spirit.

2 CORINTHIANS 3:15B–18

The golden lights of dawn brought me a new thought recently.

I was out walking early in the forest, and it was one of those dawns that bathes the world in brightness. The air looked pure gold, as if it were transparent glass. To the south of me was a whole forest of golden trees. Leaves were flakes of gold; on one tree the fruits that hung there were golden balls. And here was the strange part.

To the east, there was as yet nothing of the sun

itself—only the rising loveliness of his golden dawning. But all the beauty and gladness of spirit that came from his flaming fire!

"He makes . . . flames of fire his servants" (Psalm 104:4). I had often thought of the force of that word—the burning energy, the purging purity of flaming fire. But not of this gentler ministry, this bathing in brightness all that He touches.

The first part of that verse is this: *"He makes winds his messengers. . . ."* An old Jewish legend says that God's angels are as the winds, going and coming and ceasing to be when their service is accomplished. They are self-less servants (who ever saw a wind?); they are obedient to cause either calm or storm, fulfilling His word; and they are free (free as the wind, we say).

Isn't this a perfect picture of what you and I want to be?

Selfless.

Obedient.

Free, because we are obedient.

Cleansing in brightness all whom we touch.

Only love can be that and do that.

Lord, forevermore give us this kind of love.

THOU GIVEST—THEY GATHER: pp. 109–110

MY FATHER, TODAY . . .

   . . . transform one irritable or angry thought, to a thought and a word of love.

   . . . transform one hoarded moment, to a moment (or an hour) of patient compassion.

   . . . transform me, Father, by the little glories of this day. . . .

38

THEREFORE *I WILL*
NOT FEAR . . .

God is . . .
Therefore we will not fear, though the earth give way
and the mountains fall into the heart of the sea. . . .
The Lord Almighty is with us, the
God of Jacob is our fortress.

PSALM 46:1–2, 7

Once more, today, I hide my heart within the One who is our Refuge and Strength, "an ever present help in trouble" (Psalm 46:1).

Therefore (most blessed word!)—*therefore* I will not fear. . . .

I have seen a picture of two stone pines, on the rocky face of a mountain, so torn and ragged from the powerful gusts of wind and yet so resolutely rooted. A broken tree is not beautiful, but it shows us—God's "children in the dark storm"—which man or woman will stand, unshaken, in the Morning. . . .

There are always two pines on the mountainside of

life. Wind can blow dust in the eyes, but that dust will not blind us: ". . . yet in my flesh I will see God; I myself will see him with my own eyes—I, and not another" (Job 19:26–27).

What will it be like to see Him whom I have known so long, but never seen? To adore His beauty; to worship Him in holiness? What will it be like to see Him crowned with glory and honor, who was wounded, bruised, oppressed and afflicted *for me*? What will it be like to see *Him* and not another, not the stranger?

What will it be like . . . to see with new eyes, to hear with new ears, to know no more in part, but to know even as we are known? (1 Corinthians 13:12).

What will it be like, when faith and hope fade out of sight—and only Love is left? *What will it be like?*

For now, we do not know. Only *this* we know: The struggle and fight and sufferings of our journey are not worth comparing with the glory that will be revealed in us—in you and me!—even though we may feel we are the least of all God's redeemed children (Romans 8:18).

It is the Blessed One, and no other, who stands by us on the lonely mountain when the dark storm descends. (O my Lord, if you had not suffered, how could you help me in suffering now?) And He who suffered and overcame will grant us also to overcome.

I can think of no truer picture of what we want to be when the wind beats on us for the last time: like that lone mountain pine, broken and battered perhaps, but not uprooted!

We can stand, today and always, *steadfast, undefeated.*
And never alone.

GOLD BY MOONLIGHT: PP. 175–176

MY FATHER, SOME days, much of my personal world
seems to be shaking, and no one else even knows.... But
you know.

Thank you, Father, that when I root myself in you it
doesn't matter, even if darkness comes and my whole private world "gives way" ... for I know we'll be standing
strong ... together ... and the Morning is on its way!

39

EVERY "WINTER" COMES
TO AN END

See! The winter is past; the rains are over and gone.
Flowers appear on the earth; the season of singing has
come . . . the blossoming vines spread their fragrance.
"Arise . . . come with me."

SONG OF SONGS 2:11–13

"The Lord your God is with you. . . . He will take
great delight in you, he will [rest you] with his love, he
will rejoice over you with singing."

ZEPHANIAH 3:17

This morning, my helpers turned my chair so that I could see the leafy enclosure upon which my room opens. . . . And all this sweet greenness and dewy freshness is a message:

Leaves and flowers—down to the least bud—are nourished by the living sap within. They do not cause it to rise, or regulate its flow. They do not understand its mysterious power. But as it flows through them, it revives them. Renews them.

We may have others to help us. Or we may have no one. But whether we are set in families or must face circumstances alone, we know that we must depend on something that is not of ourselves to keep us fresh and green.

Sometimes we are too spent even to pray for this renewing life to flow within.

We need not pray! There are times when all that is asked of us is just what is asked of the leaves and flowers: They remain in the plant; the sap flows up to them:

"As the Father has loved me, so have I loved you.
Now remain in my love . . ." (John 15:9).

The most tired of us can *remain,* stay there, be there—no words can be too simple to explain what our Lord means by this: He says, simply, "Do not go away."

Even if we are completely silent, asking nothing, only letting our hearts rest in quietness in Him . . . He will cause the renewing life-sap to rise. . . .

The things we would least choose to have are round about us. But in these things, says Rutherford, "Do not let yourself be thrown down or give in to despair. Stand evenly at the will of God. . . .

"For after winter comes summer. After night comes the dawn. And after every storm, there comes clear, open skies."

ROSE FROM BRIER: PP. 61–63